Mastering the Art of Teaching: Professional Development for Experienced Teachers

Luna

Copyright © [2023]

Author: Luna

Title: Mastering the Art of Teaching: Professional Development for Experienced Teachers

All rights reserved. No part of this book may be reproduced or transmitted in any form or by any means, electronic or mechanical, including photocopying, recording, or by any information storage and retrieval system, without permission in writing from the author.

This book is a product of [Publisher's Luna]

ISBN:

TABLE OF CONTENTS

Chapter 1: The Importance of Professional Development

Chapter 1: The Importance of Professional Development

The Benefits of Continuing Education

In the ever-evolving field of education, continuing education plays a crucial role in the growth and development of experienced teachers. It provides them with the opportunity to enhance their knowledge, refine their skills, and stay up-to-date with the latest trends and advancements in the field. The benefits of continuing education are not only limited to professional growth but also have a significant impact on a teacher's effectiveness in the classroom.

One of the key benefits of continuing education is the acquisition of new knowledge. By participating in workshops, seminars, and conferences, teachers can expand their understanding of various subjects and teaching methodologies. This enables them to deepen their expertise in specific areas and improve their ability to deliver high-quality instruction. Additionally, staying informed about the latest research and best practices allows teachers to incorporate innovative and evidence-based strategies into their teaching.

Continuing education also provides teachers with the opportunity to network and collaborate with other professionals in the field. By engaging in discussions and sharing experiences with colleagues, teachers can gain new perspectives and ideas to enhance their teaching methods. Collaboration fosters creativity and encourages teachers to experiment with different approaches, ultimately leading to improved student outcomes.

Moreover, continuing education helps teachers maintain their professional licensure and certifications. Many jurisdictions require teachers to earn a certain number of professional development hours to renew their licenses. By engaging in continuing education activities, teachers can fulfill these requirements and ensure they remain qualified to teach. This not only benefits their individual careers but also contributes to the overall standard of teaching in the profession.

Continuing education also promotes personal growth and job satisfaction among teachers. By continuously learning and improving their skills, teachers can experience a sense of accomplishment and fulfillment in their profession. They become more confident in their abilities and are better equipped to handle the challenges that arise in the classroom. This, in turn, leads to increased job satisfaction and a higher level of motivation to make a positive impact on their students' lives.

In conclusion, continuing education is a vital aspect of professional development for experienced teachers. It offers numerous benefits, including the acquisition of new knowledge, networking opportunities, maintenance of professional certifications, and personal growth. By actively engaging in continuing education, teachers can enhance their teaching skills, stay current with educational trends, and ultimately provide their students with the best possible education.

Staying Up-to-Date with Teaching Techniques

In the ever-evolving field of education, it is crucial for teachers to stay up-to-date with the latest teaching techniques and methodologies. As experienced teachers, you may have already mastered the art of teaching, but that doesn't mean there isn't always room for growth and improvement. This subchapter aims to guide you on how to stay current with the ever-changing landscape of education.

One of the most effective ways to stay up-to-date with teaching techniques is by engaging in continuous professional development. By attending workshops, conferences, and seminars, you will have the opportunity to learn from experts in the field and gain new insights into effective teaching strategies. These events provide a platform for networking with other educators, allowing you to exchange ideas and learn from their experiences. Additionally, many universities and educational institutions offer online courses and certifications specifically designed for experienced teachers, enabling you to expand your knowledge and skills from the comfort of your own home.

Another valuable resource for staying current with teaching techniques is educational literature. Books, journals, and research papers provide valuable insights into the latest trends and best practices in education. By regularly reading educational publications, you can expose yourself to new ideas and innovative teaching methods. Consider joining online communities or book clubs focused on education, where you can discuss and analyze the latest publications with like-minded individuals.

Technology also plays a significant role in modern teaching techniques. As a teacher, it is essential to embrace technology and explore its potential for enhancing your teaching practices. Stay informed about the latest educational apps, online tools, and digital resources that can engage and motivate your students. Attend webinars or online courses dedicated to incorporating technology into the classroom to gain practical knowledge and skills in this area.

Lastly, never underestimate the power of collaboration. Engage in professional learning communities, both online and in-person, where you can collaborate with other educators. Share your experiences, challenges, and successes, and learn from one another. Collaborative learning allows for the exchange of ideas and fosters professional growth.

In conclusion, as experienced teachers, it is paramount to stay up-to-date with teaching techniques. Continuous professional development, reading educational literature, embracing technology, and collaborating with other educators are all effective strategies to ensure your teaching practices remain relevant and impactful. Remember, the more you invest in your professional development, the better equipped you will be to inspire and educate your students.

Developing Specializations within Teaching

In the ever-evolving field of education, teachers are constantly challenged to adapt and grow. As experienced teachers, you may find yourself seeking new opportunities to enhance your skills and knowledge. One way to achieve this is by developing specializations within teaching. This subchapter explores the benefits and strategies for pursuing specialized areas of expertise within the broader field of education.

Specializing in a particular subject or area of instruction can provide numerous advantages for both you and your students. By focusing your efforts on a specific field, you can deepen your understanding and mastery of the subject matter. This increased expertise will enable you to deliver more engaging, thorough, and effective lessons. Additionally, specializing can enhance your professional marketability, as schools often seek teachers with advanced knowledge in specific subjects.

To begin developing a specialization, it is important to identify your interests and passions within the field of education. Reflect on your teaching experiences and consider which subjects or areas have sparked your curiosity. Once you have identified your area of specialization, seek out professional development opportunities that align with your interests. This can include attending workshops, conferences, or enrolling in specialized courses or graduate programs.

Collaboration with colleagues who share similar interests can also be incredibly beneficial for developing specializations within teaching. Engage in discussions and exchange ideas with like-minded educators to expand your knowledge and gain new perspectives. Additionally, consider joining professional organizations or online communities that focus on your chosen specialization. These platforms provide opportunities for networking, sharing resources, and staying up to date with the latest developments in your field.

As you develop your specialization, it is essential to apply your newfound knowledge in the classroom. Incorporate innovative teaching strategies and resources that align with your specialized area. By doing so, you can create a more enriching and engaging learning environment for your students.

It is important to note that developing a specialization within teaching is a continuous process. As educational trends and research evolve, so should your expertise. Stay open to new ideas, embrace lifelong learning, and continually seek opportunities to expand your knowledge and skills.

In conclusion, developing specializations within teaching can be a valuable endeavor for experienced educators. By focusing on a specific subject or area of instruction, you can deepen your knowledge, enhance your teaching effectiveness, and increase your professional marketability. Embrace the journey of specialization, collaborate with colleagues, and apply your expertise in the classroom to create an exceptional learning experience for your students.

Chapter 2: Assessing Your Current Skills and Knowledge

Self-Reflection and Evaluation

In the journey of becoming a masterful teacher, self-reflection and evaluation are essential practices that will propel you towards continuous growth and improvement. As experienced teachers, you have already honed your skills and built a solid foundation in the art of teaching. However, embracing self-reflection and evaluation will allow you to take your teaching to new heights and further refine your instructional strategies.

Self-reflection is the process of looking inward and critically analyzing your own actions, decisions, and teaching practices. It involves examining your strengths and weaknesses, identifying areas for improvement, and setting goals for your professional development. By engaging in self-reflection, you gain valuable insights into your teaching style and its impact on student learning. Through this process, you can identify instructional strategies that are effective and those that may need adjustment.

Evaluation, on the other hand, involves collecting data and evidence to assess your teaching performance. This can be done through various means, such as classroom observations, student feedback, and analyzing student achievement data. By collecting and analyzing this information, you gain a comprehensive understanding of your teaching effectiveness and can make informed decisions about your instructional practices.

Self-reflection and evaluation go hand in hand, as self-reflection allows you to identify areas for evaluation, while evaluation provides feedback for self-reflection. By engaging in both practices, you can create a continuous cycle of improvement in your teaching.

To effectively engage in self-reflection and evaluation, it is important to adopt a growth mindset. Embrace the belief that you have the capacity to learn and improve, and view challenges as opportunities for growth. Be open to feedback from colleagues, administrators, and even your students, as their perspectives can provide valuable insights into your teaching.

In addition, consider incorporating self-reflection and evaluation into your daily or weekly routine. Set aside dedicated time to reflect on your teaching practices, review student work, and analyze assessment data. Keep a reflective journal or utilize digital tools to document your thoughts and observations. This will help you track your progress over time and identify patterns or areas that require attention.

Remember, self-reflection and evaluation are not meant to be judgmental or punitive. Instead, they are powerful tools for self-improvement and professional growth. By continually examining your teaching practices and seeking opportunities for growth, you will become a masterful teacher who positively impacts student learning and experiences.

Identifying Areas for Improvement

In the journey of becoming a master teacher, it is crucial to continually reflect on our practice and identify areas for improvement. As experienced teachers, we may have developed a repertoire of effective strategies and techniques over the years. However, the ever-evolving education landscape demands that we remain open to growth and adapt to the changing needs of our students. This subchapter aims to guide you, as students in the field of teacher education, on how to identify areas for improvement and take steps towards professional development.

Self-reflection is the first step in identifying areas for improvement. Take the time to critically analyze your teaching practice. Consider the strengths and weaknesses of your instructional techniques, classroom management skills, and assessment strategies. Reflecting on specific incidents and analyzing student outcomes will help you identify areas where you excel and areas that need improvement. Keep a journal or utilize reflective prompts to facilitate this process.

Seek feedback from colleagues, mentors, and even students themselves. Constructive criticism from trusted individuals can provide valuable insights into areas that may require enhancement. Consider engaging in peer observation or participating in professional learning communities to encourage collaboration and gain fresh perspectives.

Another effective method for identifying areas for improvement is through data analysis. Analyze student assessments, standardized test scores, and classroom observations to pinpoint trends and patterns.

This data-driven approach will help you identify areas where students may be struggling and allow you to tailor your instruction accordingly.

Professional development opportunities are invaluable for addressing areas of improvement. Seek out workshops, conferences, and online courses that align with your identified needs. Collaborate with colleagues or mentors to design a personalized professional development plan that targets your specific areas for growth.

Lastly, embracing a growth mindset is essential. Understand that identifying areas for improvement is a positive and necessary step towards becoming an exceptional teacher. Embrace challenges as opportunities for growth and remain open to feedback and new ideas.

In conclusion, identifying areas for improvement is a crucial aspect of professional development for experienced teachers. By engaging in self-reflection, seeking feedback, analyzing data, and pursuing professional development opportunities, you can continuously enhance your teaching practice and better meet the needs of your students. Embrace the journey of growth and mastery, and you will become a truly exceptional educator.

Setting Personal Goals for Growth

As students in the field of teacher education, it is essential to recognize the importance of personal growth throughout your professional journey. Mastering the Art of Teaching: Professional Development for Experienced Teachers is here to guide you on this path, and in this subchapter, we will explore the significance of setting personal goals for growth.

Personal goals act as a roadmap for your professional development. They allow you to focus on areas that need improvement and provide direction for your journey as an educator. By setting goals, you can enhance your teaching skills, expand your knowledge, and become a more effective teacher.

To begin, take some time to reflect on your strengths and weaknesses as a teacher. What areas of your practice do you feel confident in, and which ones could benefit from further development? Identifying these areas will help you establish meaningful goals that align with your professional needs and aspirations.

Once you have identified your strengths and weaknesses, set specific, measurable, achievable, relevant, and time-bound (SMART) goals. For example, if you feel that your classroom management skills need improvement, your SMART goal could be: "Implement and consistently reinforce a behavior management plan to decrease disruptions by 50% within the next three months." This goal is specific, measurable, achievable, relevant, and has a defined timeline, providing you with a clear target to work towards.

It is also crucial to regularly assess and evaluate your progress towards your goals. Set aside time to reflect on your practice, review your achievements, and identify areas that may require adjustments. Consider seeking feedback from mentors, colleagues, or even students, as their perspectives can offer valuable insights and help you refine your goals.

Furthermore, consider the various resources and professional development opportunities available to support your growth. Attend workshops, conferences, or webinars that align with your goals. Engage in collaborative learning by joining professional networks or participating in online communities. Take advantage of educational literature, research, and technological advancements to expand your knowledge and stay up-to-date with the latest teaching practices.

By setting personal goals for growth, you are demonstrating a commitment to continuous improvement. Embrace the process, be persistent, and celebrate your accomplishments along the way. Remember that personal growth is a lifelong journey, and each goal achieved will bring you closer to becoming an exceptional educator.

In the following chapters, we will delve deeper into specific areas of professional development, providing you with valuable insights and strategies to help you achieve your goals. Stay motivated, stay focused, and continue to strive for excellence in your teaching practice.

Chapter 3: Creating a Personalized Professional Development Plan

Identifying Relevant Resources and Opportunities

In the ever-evolving field of education, staying abreast of the latest resources and opportunities is crucial for experienced teachers who seek to enhance their professional development. This subchapter aims to equip students in the field of teacher education with the necessary tools and knowledge to identify and make the most of relevant resources and opportunities.

One of the first steps in this journey is understanding the diverse range of resources available to teachers. From textbooks and research articles to online platforms and educational apps, there are countless resources waiting to be explored. By harnessing the power of these resources, teachers can enhance their teaching methods, introduce new approaches, and keep their lessons fresh and engaging.

However, not all resources are created equal, and it is crucial for teachers to develop the ability to discern the relevance and reliability of the resources they come across. This subchapter will guide students through the process of critically evaluating resources, considering factors such as credibility, alignment with curriculum standards, and applicability to their specific teaching context. By honing these skills, teachers can make informed decisions about which resources to integrate into their lesson plans and instructional practices.

Beyond resources, this subchapter also emphasizes the importance of identifying and seizing opportunities for professional growth.

Teachers must be proactive in seeking out opportunities for collaboration, networking, and ongoing learning. Whether it's attending conferences and workshops, joining professional organizations, or participating in online communities, teachers can benefit greatly from connecting with like-minded educators who can share insights, experiences, and best practices.

Additionally, this subchapter encourages students to explore opportunities for professional development within their own schools and districts. From mentoring programs and job shadowing to curriculum development committees and leadership roles, there are numerous avenues for growth and advancement within the teaching profession. By actively seeking out these opportunities, teachers can enhance their skills, take on new challenges, and contribute to the development of their educational community.

In conclusion, "Identifying Relevant Resources and Opportunities" is a subchapter that aims to empower students in the field of teacher education by equipping them with the necessary skills to identify and make the most of relevant resources and opportunities. By mastering the art of resource evaluation and actively seeking out opportunities for growth, teachers can continuously enhance their teaching practice and contribute to the advancement of the field of education.

Balancing Time and Commitments

In the fast-paced world of teaching, finding a balance between time and commitments can often feel like an elusive goal. As experienced teachers, we understand the demands that come with the profession. From lesson planning and grading papers to attending meetings and extracurricular activities, our days can quickly become consumed by the needs of our students and schools. However, it is essential to remember that finding a healthy balance between our professional and personal lives is crucial for our own well-being and effectiveness as educators.

One key aspect of balancing time and commitments is effective time management. As teachers, we must learn to prioritize our tasks and allocate our time efficiently. Creating a schedule or a to-do list can be immensely helpful in organizing our days and ensuring that we complete essential tasks in a timely manner. By setting realistic goals and deadlines, we can avoid feeling overwhelmed and make the most of our time.

Additionally, it is essential to set boundaries and learn to say no. While we have a passion for our work and a desire to help our students succeed, it is important to recognize our limitations. Taking on too many commitments can lead to burnout and a decline in the quality of our teaching. Learning to prioritize and politely decline tasks that are not essential to our role as educators is an important skill to develop.

Furthermore, finding time for ourselves and our personal lives is crucial for maintaining a healthy work-life balance. Engaging in hobbies, spending time with loved ones, and taking care of our physical and mental well-being are all essential components of being a well-rounded and effective teacher. By taking care of ourselves, we can better serve our students and bring our best selves to the classroom.

Lastly, seeking support and collaboration from colleagues can greatly alleviate the burden of balancing time and commitments. Building a network of trusted colleagues and mentors can provide a sounding board for ideas, offer assistance, and share the workload. By working together, we can create a supportive community that understands the unique challenges and demands of the teaching profession.

In conclusion, finding a balance between time and commitments is a constant challenge for experienced teachers. By implementing effective time management strategies, setting boundaries, prioritizing self-care, and seeking support from colleagues, we can strive for a healthier work-life balance. Remember, taking care of ourselves is not only beneficial for our well-being but also for the success of our students.

Seeking Support and Collaboration

As experienced teachers, we know that the journey of mastering the art of teaching is a lifelong process. It is through continuous learning and seeking support and collaboration that we can grow both personally and professionally. In this subchapter, we will explore the importance of seeking support and collaboration in the field of teacher education.

One of the most valuable resources for any teacher is the support of their peers. By collaborating with other educators, we can share ideas, strategies, and experiences that can enhance our teaching practices. Collaboration allows us to tap into a collective wisdom, drawing from a diverse pool of expertise and perspectives. Whether it is through formal professional learning communities or informal conversations with colleagues, the power of collaboration should not be underestimated.

Furthermore, seeking support from mentors or coaches can be invaluable in our professional development. These experienced individuals can provide guidance, feedback, and encouragement as we navigate the challenges of the teaching profession. They can offer insights into effective teaching practices, help us reflect on our own teaching methods, and provide a fresh perspective on classroom dynamics. By engaging in a mentorship or coaching relationship, we can gain valuable insights and support that will ultimately benefit our students.

In addition to seeking support within our immediate circles, it is essential to take advantage of the broader community of educators. Attending conferences, workshops, and seminars can expose us to new ideas, research, and best practices in the field of teacher education. These events provide opportunities to network with like-minded professionals, engage in meaningful discussions, and gain inspiration from the work of others. By actively participating in these communities, we can stay up-to-date with the latest trends and research, and continually refine our teaching methods.

Lastly, seeking support and collaboration also extends to our students. By fostering a collaborative classroom environment, we encourage our students to work together, share ideas, and support one another. This not only enhances their learning experience but also creates a sense of community and belonging. By encouraging collaboration among students, we are preparing them for the collaborative nature of the 21st-century workforce.

In conclusion, seeking support and collaboration is essential for professional development in the field of teacher education. By collaborating with peers, seeking mentorship, participating in professional communities, and fostering collaboration among students, we can continue to grow and refine our teaching practices. The journey of mastering the art of teaching is not a solitary one but rather a collective endeavor, where support and collaboration play a vital role in our success as educators.

Chapter 4: Engaging in Collaborative Professional Development

Joining Professional Learning Communities

In the world of education, professional development plays a crucial role in enhancing the skills and knowledge of experienced teachers. One of the most effective ways to engage in continuous learning is by joining professional learning communities (PLCs). This subchapter will delve into the significance of joining PLCs, the benefits it offers, and how it can contribute to the growth and success of teachers in the field of education.

A professional learning community is a group of educators who come together voluntarily to collaborate, share ideas, and engage in reflective discussions about pedagogy, student learning, and instructional practices. PLCs provide a supportive and collaborative environment where teachers can learn from one another, exchange best practices, and discuss challenges they face in their classrooms.

Joining a professional learning community offers numerous benefits for teachers. Firstly, it provides opportunities for professional growth and development. By interacting with fellow educators and sharing experiences, teachers can expand their knowledge base, gain new perspectives, and stay updated with the latest research and trends in education.

PLCs also foster a sense of belonging and camaraderie among teachers. It creates a supportive network where teachers can seek advice, share successes, and find solutions to common challenges. Engaging in discussions with like-minded educators can be inspiring and motivating, reinvigorating teachers' passion for teaching.

Furthermore, PLCs promote reflective teaching practices. By regularly engaging in discussions and reflecting on their own teaching strategies, teachers can gain valuable insights into their strengths and areas for improvement. This reflective process enables teachers to refine their instructional techniques, leading to enhanced student learning outcomes.

Joining a professional learning community is especially relevant for students pursuing teacher education. As aspiring teachers, being part of a PLC can provide valuable exposure to the realities of teaching, insights into best practices, and a platform to discuss educational theories. It can help students bridge the gap between theory and practice, preparing them for the challenges they may face in their future classrooms.

In conclusion, joining professional learning communities is a vital component of professional development for experienced teachers and teacher education students. These communities offer a supportive environment for collaboration, professional growth, and reflective practices. By joining a PLC, teachers can enhance their teaching skills, gain new perspectives, and build a strong network of like-minded professionals. Whether you are an experienced teacher or a student aspiring to become one, joining a professional learning community will undoubtedly contribute to your growth and success in the field of education.

Participating in Workshops and Conferences

In the ever-evolving field of education, continuous professional development is essential for experienced teachers to stay updated with the latest teaching methodologies, strategies, and research findings. One of the most effective ways to enhance your teaching skills and broaden your knowledge is by participating in workshops and conferences. These events provide a unique platform for teachers to network, learn from experts in the field, and exchange ideas with peers.

Workshops and conferences offer a wide range of topics and themes related to teacher education. Whether you are interested in classroom management, differentiated instruction, or integrating technology into your lessons, you are likely to find a workshop or conference that suits your needs. These events are designed to provide practical ideas, strategies, and resources that can be immediately implemented in your classroom, making your teaching more effective and engaging.

Attending workshops and conferences also allows you to interact with fellow teachers from different schools and districts. This networking opportunity is invaluable as it opens doors to collaboration, sharing of best practices, and building a support system within the teaching community. By engaging in conversations with like-minded educators, you can gain insights, ideas, and perspectives that can inspire and transform your teaching practice.

Furthermore, workshops and conferences often invite renowned experts in the field of education as keynote speakers or presenters. Listening to their experiences, research findings, and success stories can be a source of inspiration and motivation. These experts often share innovative approaches and practices that can challenge your existing teaching methods and encourage you to explore new avenues in your classroom.

To make the most of workshops and conferences, it is important to come prepared. Prioritize the sessions that align with your professional goals and interests. Take notes, ask questions, and actively participate in discussions. Engage with other attendees during breaks and networking sessions to expand your professional network. Lastly, reflect on your learnings and identify how you can apply them in your teaching practice.

In conclusion, participating in workshops and conferences is a vital aspect of professional development for experienced teachers. These events provide opportunities to learn, grow, and connect with others in the field of education. By taking advantage of these platforms, you can enhance your teaching skills, stay current with educational trends, and ultimately, improve student learning outcomes.

Collaborating with Colleagues for Mutual Growth

In the field of education, collaboration is a key component for professional growth and development. As experienced teachers, it is essential to recognize the value of working together with our colleagues to enhance our teaching practices and ultimately improve student outcomes. This subchapter delves into the importance of collaborating with colleagues and provides practical strategies for fostering mutual growth in a teacher education context.

One of the primary benefits of collaborating with colleagues is the opportunity for shared knowledge and expertise. Each teacher brings unique skills and experiences to the table, and by collaborating, we can tap into this collective wisdom. Engaging in discussions, exchanging ideas, and seeking feedback from fellow teachers can offer fresh perspectives and innovative approaches to teaching. This collaborative environment not only benefits individual teachers but also cultivates a culture of continuous learning within the educational community.

Furthermore, collaborating with colleagues fosters a sense of camaraderie and support. Teaching can sometimes be a solitary profession, with teachers spending most of their time in their own classrooms. However, by actively seeking opportunities to collaborate, we can break down these barriers and build a network of support. Engaging in professional learning communities, attending workshops, or participating in collaborative projects can create a sense of belonging and shared purpose. Together, we can overcome challenges, share successes, and inspire each other to grow as professionals.

To foster collaboration with colleagues for mutual growth, it is crucial to establish a culture of trust and respect. Creating an environment where teachers feel safe to share their ideas and concerns is paramount. Encouraging open communication, active listening, and providing constructive feedback are essential elements for effective collaboration. Additionally, setting clear goals and objectives for collaborative projects can help ensure that everyone is working towards a common purpose.

In conclusion, collaboration with colleagues is an invaluable tool for ongoing professional development in the field of education. By working together, sharing knowledge, and supporting one another, we can enhance our teaching practices and ultimately improve student learning outcomes. As experienced teachers, it is essential to actively seek opportunities for collaboration, establish a culture of trust and respect, and embrace the collective wisdom of our colleagues. By doing so, we can continue to master the art of teaching and make a positive impact on our students' lives.

Chapter 5: Utilizing Technology for Professional Development

Exploring Online Learning Platforms

In today's digital age, online learning platforms have revolutionized the way we acquire knowledge and skills. As aspiring teachers, it is crucial for you to understand and utilize these platforms to enhance your professional development. This subchapter will delve into the world of online learning platforms, their benefits, and how you can make the most out of them in your teacher education journey.

Online learning platforms offer a wide range of courses and resources specifically designed for teachers. These platforms provide flexibility, allowing you to learn at your own pace and convenience. You can access a variety of courses, workshops, and webinars focused on different aspects of teaching, including classroom management, curriculum development, instructional strategies, and assessment techniques. By exploring these platforms, you can gain valuable insights from experienced educators and experts in the field, expanding your knowledge base and refining your teaching skills.

One of the key advantages of online learning platforms is the opportunity for networking and collaboration. These platforms often offer discussion forums, virtual communities, and social media groups where you can connect with fellow teachers from around the world. Engaging in these communities allows you to share ideas, seek advice, and collaborate on projects, fostering a global perspective on education. By leveraging the power of online learning platforms, you can build a strong professional network and establish meaningful connections with like-minded educators.

To get the most out of online learning platforms, it is important to approach them with a strategic mindset. Start by setting clear goals and objectives for your professional development. Identify specific areas of teaching that you want to improve upon and seek out relevant courses and resources on the platforms. Create a schedule and allocate dedicated time for online learning, ensuring a consistent and focused approach.

Additionally, actively participate in the online communities offered by these platforms. Engage in discussions, ask questions, and contribute your own insights and experiences. By actively engaging in these communities, you can enhance your learning experience and gain practical knowledge from other teachers.

In conclusion, online learning platforms are powerful tools for professional development in teacher education. They offer flexibility, a wealth of resources, and networking opportunities that can greatly enhance your teaching skills. By exploring these platforms and utilizing them effectively, you can master the art of teaching and become a more confident and effective educator. Embrace the digital age and embark on a journey of continuous learning through online platforms to excel in your teaching career.

Engaging in Webinars and Virtual Conferences

In the ever-evolving field of education, it is crucial for teachers to continually enhance their skills and stay up-to-date with the latest teaching methodologies and technologies. With the advent of webinars and virtual conferences, professional development opportunities have become more accessible and convenient than ever before. This subchapter aims to guide students in the field of teacher education on how to effectively engage in webinars and virtual conferences to maximize their professional growth.

Webinars and virtual conferences offer a wealth of benefits for experienced teachers seeking to expand their knowledge and refine their teaching practices. These online platforms provide opportunities to learn from experts in the field, gain insights into innovative teaching strategies, and connect with like-minded professionals from all over the world. By participating in webinars and virtual conferences, teachers can stay at the forefront of educational advancements and bring fresh ideas into their classrooms.

To make the most of these virtual learning experiences, it is important for students to approach them with a proactive mindset. Before attending a webinar or virtual conference, students should thoroughly research the topic and speakers to ensure the content aligns with their professional goals. They should also come prepared with questions or topics they wish to explore further during the session. Active engagement during these online events can lead to more meaningful learning experiences and facilitate networking opportunities with other educators.

During webinars and virtual conferences, students should embrace the interactive features provided by the platform. Most virtual learning platforms offer chat boxes or Q&A sessions where participants can engage with presenters and fellow attendees. Students should take advantage of these features to ask questions, share their thoughts, and collaborate with others. Actively participating in discussions not only enhances learning but also helps build a professional network of like-minded educators.

After attending a webinar or virtual conference, students should reflect on their learning experiences and identify key takeaways. It is essential to apply the knowledge gained from these sessions to their own classrooms and teaching practices. Sharing insights and lessons learned with colleagues or through online platforms can further contribute to the professional growth of all educators involved.

Engaging in webinars and virtual conferences is a powerful tool for experienced teachers to continue their professional development journey. By actively participating and applying the knowledge gained, students in teacher education can master the art of teaching and become more effective educators in their classrooms.

Leveraging Social Media for Professional Networking

In today's digital age, social media has become an integral part of our daily lives. It has not only revolutionized the way we connect with friends and family but has also opened up new avenues for professional networking. As aspiring educators, harnessing the power of social media can greatly enhance your career prospects and open doors to endless opportunities in the field of teaching.

Social media platforms such as LinkedIn, Twitter, and Facebook provide unique spaces for teachers and educators to connect with like-minded professionals, share resources, and engage in meaningful discussions. These platforms offer a virtual networking space that transcends geographical boundaries, allowing you to connect with educators from around the world. By actively participating in online communities, you can expand your professional network, gain insights from experienced educators, and stay up-to-date with the latest trends and innovations in the field of education.

LinkedIn, often referred to as the "professional Facebook," is particularly valuable for teachers. It serves as an online resume, showcasing your qualifications, experience, and skills to potential employers. By joining education-related groups, you can engage in discussions, share ideas, and even connect with recruiters looking for passionate educators like yourself. Additionally, LinkedIn offers job search features that allow you to explore various teaching positions and connect with schools or organizations that align with your career goals.

Twitter, on the other hand, is a powerful platform for professional development. By following education-focused accounts and participating in educational chats, you can access a wealth of resources, lesson plans, and teaching strategies shared by experienced educators. Twitter also provides an opportunity to engage in conversations with educational thought leaders, allowing you to learn from their expertise and broaden your perspectives.

Facebook groups dedicated to teacher education are another valuable resource. These communities provide a platform for educators to collaborate, seek advice, and share experiences. By actively participating in these groups, you can tap into a vast network of educators who can provide guidance, support, and inspiration throughout your teaching journey.

However, it is important to remember that maintaining a professional online presence is crucial. Ensure that your social media profiles reflect your dedication to education and professionalism. Avoid posting controversial or inappropriate content that could potentially harm your reputation. Instead, share educational insights, resources, and experiences that demonstrate your passion for teaching.

In conclusion, social media has become an indispensable tool for professional networking in the field of education. By leveraging platforms such as LinkedIn, Twitter, and Facebook, you can connect with educators worldwide, access valuable resources, and expand your knowledge and skills. Embrace the power of social media and unlock a world of opportunities as you embark on your teaching career.

Chapter 6: Incorporating Research-Based Practices into Teaching

Staying Informed about Current Educational Research

In the ever-evolving field of education, staying up-to-date with the latest research and best practices is crucial for teachers to provide the highest quality education to their students. As experienced teachers, you have already mastered the art of teaching, but continuous learning is essential to ensure that you are equipped with the latest knowledge and strategies to address the diverse needs of your students.

This subchapter aims to guide you on how to stay informed about current educational research, enabling you to enhance your teaching methods and improve student outcomes. Here are some valuable strategies to consider:

1. Subscribe to reputable educational journals and publications: Numerous journals and publications focus on educational research, offering valuable insights and summaries of recent studies. By subscribing to these resources, you can access articles and research findings that are relevant to your teaching practice.

2. Attend professional development workshops and conferences: Teacher education is a lifelong journey, and attending workshops and conferences is an excellent way to stay informed about the latest research and trends in education. These events provide opportunities to learn from leading experts, collaborate with fellow educators, and gain new perspectives on teaching methodologies.

3. Engage in online communities and forums: The internet provides a wealth of resources for educators. Joining online communities and forums dedicated to teacher education enables you to connect with like-minded professionals and engage in discussions about current research. These platforms often share links to research papers, blogs, and other relevant resources.

4. Collaborate with colleagues: Your fellow teachers can be valuable sources of information and insights. Engage in regular discussions with colleagues to share knowledge and experiences. Collaborative planning sessions and peer observations can also provide opportunities to learn from each other and incorporate research-based strategies into your teaching.

5. Follow educational research organizations and experts on social media: Social media platforms like Twitter and LinkedIn offer a convenient way to stay informed about educational research. Follow reputable research organizations, education experts, and influential educators to receive updates on the latest studies, trends, and innovative teaching practices.

By actively engaging in these strategies, you can ensure that your teaching practice remains current, evidence-based, and student-centered. Embracing the concept of lifelong learning is essential for experienced teachers, as it allows you to continuously refine your skills and adapt your teaching methods to meet the changing needs of your students.

Remember, staying informed about current educational research is not only beneficial for your own professional growth but also for the success and well-being of your students. By incorporating evidence-based practices, you can create a positive and engaging learning environment that empowers your students to thrive academically and personally.

Implementing Evidence-Based Strategies in the Classroom

As aspiring teachers, it is crucial to understand the significance of evidence-based strategies in the classroom. In the ever-evolving landscape of education, it is imperative to stay current with research-backed methods that have been proven to enhance student learning and achievement. This subchapter will delve into the importance of implementing evidence-based strategies in the classroom and provide practical tips for incorporating them into your teaching practice.

Why are evidence-based strategies important? Simply put, these strategies are grounded in research and have been shown to be effective in promoting student learning. By utilizing evidence-based strategies, you are ensuring that your instructional methods are based on sound educational principles rather than relying solely on personal beliefs or anecdotal evidence. This approach ensures that you are equipped with the most effective tools to engage your students and foster their academic growth.

One key aspect of implementing evidence-based strategies is understanding the research behind them. Stay updated on current studies and research findings in the field of education. This will enable you to identify strategies that align with your teaching goals and the needs of your students. It is also important to critically evaluate research and consider its applicability to your specific classroom context.

When implementing evidence-based strategies, it is crucial to consider the diverse needs and backgrounds of your students. Take into account their individual learning styles, abilities, and cultural backgrounds. Differentiate your instruction to accommodate various learning needs and provide equitable opportunities for all students to succeed.

Collaboration and professional development are essential components of implementing evidence-based strategies. Engage in discussions and collaborations with your colleagues to share ideas and best practices. Attend workshops, conferences, and webinars that focus on evidence-based teaching strategies. This continuous professional development will enhance your knowledge and skills, enabling you to implement effective strategies in your classroom.

Lastly, don't be afraid to experiment and reflect on the outcomes of your teaching strategies. Actively seek feedback from your students and colleagues. Reflect on the strengths and weaknesses of your instructional practices and make necessary adjustments. By adopting a growth mindset, you will be able to refine your teaching methods and continuously improve as an educator.

In conclusion, implementing evidence-based strategies in the classroom is crucial for enhancing student learning and achievement. By staying informed about current research, differentiating instruction, collaborating with colleagues, and reflecting on your teaching practice, you will be well-equipped to provide an engaging and effective learning environment for your students. Embrace evidence-based strategies as a cornerstone of your teaching practice and watch your students thrive.

Adapting Teaching Techniques to Individual Student Needs

In the ever-evolving landscape of education, it is essential for teachers to recognize and respond to the unique needs of each student in their classroom. As experienced educators, we understand that every learner is different, with varying abilities, interests, and learning styles. This subchapter aims to provide you, as student-teachers, with strategies to adapt your teaching techniques to meet the individual needs of your students.

The first step in adapting your teaching techniques is to gain a deep understanding of your students. Take the time to connect with each learner and get to know their strengths, weaknesses, and interests. This can be done through informal conversations, diagnostic assessments, and observation. By understanding their abilities and personal motivations, you can tailor your teaching approach to engage and challenge them effectively.

One method to adapt teaching techniques is through differentiation. This involves modifying the content, process, or product of instruction to suit the needs of different students. For example, you can provide alternative reading materials at different levels of difficulty, offer varied assignments that allow for multiple ways of demonstrating understanding, or incorporate technology to accommodate different learning styles.

Another approach is to utilize flexible grouping strategies. Grouping students based on their abilities and learning preferences can create a more personalized learning experience. This may involve small group work, peer tutoring, or one-on-one instruction. By grouping students strategically, you can provide targeted support and challenge, helping each student achieve their full potential.

Furthermore, incorporating formative assessments into your teaching can enable you to monitor student progress and adjust your instruction accordingly. Regularly assessing student understanding and providing timely feedback allows for ongoing adjustment of your teaching techniques to meet the individual needs of your students. This can involve using exit slips, quizzes, or other informal assessment tools to gather feedback on student learning.

In conclusion, adapting teaching techniques to individual student needs is a critical aspect of effective teaching. By recognizing and responding to the unique abilities and interests of your students, you can create a learning environment that fosters growth and success. By implementing strategies such as differentiation, flexible grouping, and formative assessments, you can ensure that each student receives the support and challenge they require. Remember, mastering the art of teaching requires continuous reflection and adaptation to meet the diverse needs of your students.

Chapter 7: Reflecting on Teaching Practices

The Power of Reflective Practice

In the field of education, there is a growing recognition of the power of reflective practice for professional development. As experienced teachers, it is crucial for us to engage in this self-reflective process to enhance our teaching skills and improve student outcomes. This subchapter will explore the importance of reflective practice and provide practical strategies for implementing it in our daily teaching practice.

Reflective practice involves intentionally stepping back from our teaching experiences and critically examining our actions, decisions, and their impact on student learning. By engaging in this process, we can gain valuable insights into our strengths and areas for improvement, leading to continuous growth as educators.

One of the key benefits of reflective practice is its ability to enhance our self-awareness. By taking the time to reflect on our teaching practices, we can develop a deeper understanding of our teaching philosophy, beliefs, and values. This self-awareness enables us to align our teaching strategies with our goals and values, creating a more authentic and meaningful learning experience for our students.

Reflective practice also allows us to identify and address any gaps in our knowledge and skills. By reflecting on our teaching experiences, we can recognize areas where we may need further professional development or additional resources. This self-assessment enables us to continuously improve our instructional practices and stay updated with the latest research and best practices in education.

Furthermore, reflective practice helps us make informed decisions about our teaching strategies. By critically analyzing our actions and their impact on student learning, we can make adjustments and adaptations to our instruction to better meet the diverse needs of our students. This reflective process promotes a culture of continuous improvement, where we constantly strive to provide the most effective and engaging learning experiences for our students.

To implement reflective practice in our teaching, we can adopt various strategies. One approach is to keep a reflective journal, where we document our thoughts, experiences, and insights about our teaching practice. This journal can serve as a valuable resource for future reference and reflection.

Additionally, engaging in peer observation and feedback can greatly enhance our reflective practice. By observing our colleagues' teaching and receiving constructive feedback, we can gain new perspectives and fresh ideas for our own teaching practice.

In conclusion, the power of reflective practice cannot be underestimated in the field of education. As experienced teachers, engaging in this self-reflective process allows us to enhance our self-awareness, address gaps in our knowledge and skills, make informed decisions about our teaching strategies, and continuously improve our instructional practices. By implementing reflective practice, we can become more effective and impactful educators, ultimately benefiting our students and their learning outcomes.

Seeking Feedback from Students and Colleagues

As experienced teachers, we have all reached a point in our careers where we feel confident in our abilities and techniques. However, it is crucial to remember that there is always room for growth and improvement. Seeking feedback from our students and colleagues is an essential part of our professional development journey.

When we ask for feedback from our students, we gain valuable insights into their learning experiences. By giving them a voice, we empower them to take an active role in their education. Students can provide us with unique perspectives and suggestions that we may not have considered before. Their feedback can help us identify areas where we can make adjustments or introduce new strategies to enhance their learning.

To effectively seek feedback from our students, we need to create a safe and supportive environment where they feel comfortable sharing their thoughts. We can use various methods such as anonymous surveys, one-on-one conversations, or group discussions to gather their insights. By demonstrating that we genuinely value their opinions, we encourage them to provide honest and constructive feedback.

In addition to seeking feedback from our students, it is equally important to engage in conversations with our colleagues. Colleagues can offer valuable insights and suggestions based on their own experiences and expertise. By sharing our successes and challenges with each other, we can learn from one another and develop a more comprehensive understanding of effective teaching practices.

To foster a culture of feedback within our professional community, we can organize regular meetings or workshops where teachers can discuss their teaching methods and exchange ideas. Collaborative lesson planning sessions can also provide opportunities for colleagues to observe each other's classes and provide constructive feedback. Through these interactions, we can establish a supportive network that promotes continuous growth and improvement.

Ultimately, seeking feedback from our students and colleagues allows us to become more reflective practitioners. It enables us to identify our strengths and areas for improvement, leading to enhanced teaching practices and student learning outcomes. As experienced teachers, it is our responsibility to create an environment that encourages feedback and fosters a culture of continuous professional development.

In conclusion, seeking feedback from students and colleagues is an integral part of mastering the art of teaching. By actively listening to our students and engaging in collaborative discussions with our colleagues, we can refine our teaching strategies, improve student learning experiences, and ultimately become more effective educators. Let us embrace the power of feedback and continue to grow and evolve in our profession.

Adjusting Instruction based on Reflection and Feedback

As experienced teachers, it is crucial for us to continually reflect on our teaching practices and seek feedback in order to enhance our instructional strategies. This subchapter will delve into the importance of adjusting instruction based on reflection and feedback, providing you, as students of teacher education, with valuable insights into professional development.

Reflection plays a vital role in our growth as educators. Taking the time to critically analyze our teaching methods, classroom management techniques, and student outcomes allows us to identify areas of improvement. By engaging in self-reflection, we can pinpoint our strengths and weaknesses, enabling us to make necessary adjustments in our instruction.

Feedback, both from students and colleagues, is another invaluable tool for professional development. Students provide valuable insights into the effectiveness of our teaching methods and strategies. By actively seeking feedback from our students, we can gain a better understanding of their learning needs and adjust our instruction accordingly. Likewise, collaborating with colleagues and participating in peer evaluations can offer fresh perspectives and innovative ideas that can significantly enhance our teaching practices.

One effective approach to adjusting instruction based on reflection and feedback is the use of formative assessments. By regularly assessing student progress and understanding, we can identify areas where our teaching may need adjustment. Formative assessments allow us to gather real-time data on student learning, enabling us to adapt our instruction to meet the specific needs of our students.

In this subchapter, we will explore various strategies for adjusting instruction based on reflection and feedback. We will discuss the importance of creating a culture of reflection in our classrooms, where students are encouraged to provide feedback and actively participate in their own learning journey. Additionally, we will delve into the process of analyzing assessment data and using it to inform our instructional decisions.

By mastering the art of adjusting instruction based on reflection and feedback, we can become more effective educators. This subchapter aims to equip you, as students of teacher education, with the necessary tools and insights to continuously grow and improve as teachers. Embracing reflection and feedback as integral parts of our professional development will ultimately lead to enhanced student outcomes and a more fulfilling teaching experience.

Chapter 8: Balancing Professional Development with Work-Life Balance

Prioritizing Self-Care and Well-being

In the fast-paced world of teaching, it is easy for educators to neglect their own self-care and well-being. As experienced teachers, we often devote all our energy and time to our students, forgetting that we also need to take care of ourselves. This subchapter aims to shed light on the importance of prioritizing self-care and well-being and provides practical strategies for maintaining a healthy work-life balance.

Teaching is a demanding profession that requires teachers to give their best every day. However, it is crucial to remember that we cannot pour from an empty cup. Taking care of ourselves is not selfish; it is a necessary step towards becoming effective and fulfilled educators. When we prioritize self-care and well-being, we are better equipped to handle the challenges of the classroom and provide the best learning experiences for our students.

One key aspect of self-care and well-being is managing stress. Teaching can be stressful, but it is essential to find healthy ways to cope with it. This subchapter explores various stress management techniques, such as practicing mindfulness, engaging in physical exercise, and developing a support network. By implementing these strategies, teachers can reduce stress levels and increase their overall well-being.

Furthermore, maintaining a healthy work-life balance is crucial for teachers. It is easy to get caught up in the never-ending cycle of lesson planning, grading, and extracurricular activities. However, neglecting personal interests and relationships can lead to burnout and dissatisfaction. This subchapter delves into strategies for setting boundaries, time management, and creating space for personal hobbies and social connections. By striking a balance between work and personal life, teachers can sustain their passion and enthusiasm for the profession.

Finally, this subchapter emphasizes the significance of self-reflection and professional growth. Engaging in continuous learning and self-improvement not only benefits teachers but also enhances the educational experiences of their students. By seeking out professional development opportunities, teachers can stay up-to-date with current pedagogical practices and expand their knowledge and skills.

In conclusion, prioritizing self-care and well-being is essential for experienced teachers. This subchapter provides valuable insights and practical strategies for achieving a healthy work-life balance, managing stress, and fostering personal growth. By taking care of ourselves, we can continue to inspire and guide our students effectively, creating a positive and empowering learning environment.

Time Management Strategies for Continuous Learning

In the fast-paced world of education, teachers are constantly juggling multiple responsibilities and demands on their time. From lesson planning and grading papers to attending professional development workshops and meetings, it can often feel overwhelming. However, mastering the art of time management is crucial for teachers who wish to continue their professional development and grow in their careers. This subchapter will explore effective time management strategies specifically tailored for teachers in the field of education.

One of the fundamental strategies for time management is prioritization. By identifying the most important tasks and focusing on them first, teachers can ensure that they are utilizing their time efficiently. Creating a to-do list, either on paper or digitally, can help teachers stay organized and ensure they are not missing any critical tasks.

Another strategy is setting clear goals and deadlines. By breaking down larger tasks into smaller, manageable chunks, teachers can avoid feeling overwhelmed and maintain a sense of progress. Setting deadlines for each task can also help teachers stay accountable and motivated.

Effective time management also includes avoiding procrastination. Teachers should identify their most productive times of the day and schedule their most challenging tasks during these periods. By tackling difficult tasks when they have the most energy and focus, teachers can maximize their productivity.

Additionally, avoiding multitasking is crucial for effective time management. While it may seem like multitasking can increase productivity, research has shown that it actually leads to decreased efficiency and increased errors. Instead, teachers should focus on one task at a time, completing it thoroughly before moving on to the next.

Furthermore, establishing boundaries and learning to say no can be essential for time management. Teachers often find themselves faced with numerous requests and obligations, but it is important to recognize their limitations and prioritize their own well-being. By setting boundaries and learning to say no when necessary, teachers can protect their time and energy for the tasks that truly matter.

In conclusion, time management is a vital skill for teachers in the field of education, especially when it comes to continuous learning and professional development. By implementing strategies such as prioritization, goal setting, avoiding procrastination, staying focused on one task at a time, and establishing boundaries, teachers can effectively manage their time and make the most of their professional growth opportunities. By mastering the art of time management, teachers can enhance their teaching practices and ultimately achieve greater success in their careers.

Achieving Work-Life Balance as an Experienced Teacher

As an experienced teacher, you have undoubtedly dedicated countless hours to honing your craft and providing the best education for your students. However, it is crucial to remember that maintaining a healthy work-life balance is equally important for your overall well-being and effectiveness as an educator. In this subchapter, we will explore strategies and tips for achieving work-life balance as an experienced teacher.

First and foremost, it is essential to set boundaries between your personal and professional life. Often, experienced teachers find themselves constantly thinking about lesson plans, grading papers, and responding to emails even after school hours. While dedication to your profession is admirable, it is crucial to carve out time for yourself and your loved ones. Consider establishing specific times for work-related tasks and stick to them. For instance, designate a specific time in the evening to respond to emails, and once that time is over, focus solely on your personal life.

Another strategy to achieve work-life balance is to prioritize self-care. As a teacher, you are constantly giving to others, and it is easy to neglect your own needs. However, remember that you cannot pour from an empty cup. Make time for activities that bring you joy and relaxation, whether it's pursuing a hobby, exercising, or simply spending quality time with loved ones. By taking care of yourself, you will be better equipped to handle the demands of your profession.

Additionally, consider seeking support from your colleagues and administration. Experienced teachers can often feel overwhelmed by the weight of their responsibilities. Reach out to fellow educators for advice and support. Sharing experiences and collaborating with others can alleviate stress and provide new perspectives. Furthermore, communicate with your administration about your workload and potential areas where you may need assistance. Open and honest communication can lead to a more balanced workload and a healthier work environment.

Finally, embrace the power of saying no. As an experienced teacher, you may feel obligated to take on additional responsibilities or participate in every extracurricular activity. However, it is crucial to recognize your limits and prioritize your well-being. Learn to say no to tasks or commitments that do not align with your goals or values. By doing so, you will free up time and energy to focus on what truly matters.

In conclusion, achieving work-life balance as an experienced teacher is crucial for your personal and professional well-being. By setting boundaries, prioritizing self-care, seeking support, and learning to say no, you can create a harmonious and fulfilling life both inside and outside the classroom. Remember, taking care of yourself is just as important as taking care of your students.

Chapter 9: Navigating Professional Development Opportunities

Seeking Grants and Scholarships for Professional Growth

In the ever-evolving field of education, continuous professional growth is essential for teachers to stay updated with the latest techniques, research, and trends. However, pursuing professional development can be costly, especially for experienced teachers who may have limited financial resources. Thankfully, there are numerous grants and scholarships available specifically for teacher education, offering financial assistance to support your journey towards mastering the art of teaching.

Grants and scholarships are valuable resources for teachers seeking to enhance their knowledge and skills. They provide financial aid that can cover various expenses, such as tuition fees, course materials, travel costs, and even living expenses during the duration of the program. These opportunities are typically awarded based on merit, financial need, or a combination of both.

To begin your search for grants and scholarships, it is important to start by exploring local, regional, and national organizations that support teacher education. Many professional associations, foundations, and government agencies offer funding opportunities specifically for educators. These organizations understand the importance of continuous professional development and are eager to invest in the growth of dedicated teachers like yourself.

When applying for grants and scholarships, it is crucial to carefully review the eligibility criteria and requirements. Each opportunity may have specific prerequisites, such as years of teaching experience, grade level focus, or subject area expertise. Make sure to tailor your application to highlight your unique qualifications and the ways in which the funding will impact your professional growth.

Additionally, consider reaching out to your school district or local education agency for potential funding opportunities. Some districts may have their own grants or scholarships available exclusively for their teachers. By networking with colleagues and administrators, you may gain access to information about hidden gems that can support your professional development.

Furthermore, do not underestimate the power of online resources. Many websites and databases compile comprehensive lists of grants and scholarships for teacher education. These platforms allow you to filter opportunities based on your specific needs and interests, making the search process more efficient and effective.

Remember, seeking grants and scholarships for professional growth requires persistence and dedication. Be proactive in your search, stay organized, and submit applications well in advance of the deadlines. By investing time and effort into securing funding, you are investing in your own growth as an educator and ultimately, the success of your students.

In conclusion, grants and scholarships are invaluable resources for experienced teachers seeking to continue their professional development journey. By exploring local, regional, and national opportunities, tailoring your applications, and utilizing online resources, you can find the financial support you need to master the art of teaching. Embrace the opportunity to pursue your passion and invest in your growth as an educator, for the benefit of both yourself and your students.

Exploring Advanced Degree Programs and Certifications

As an experienced teacher, you have already mastered the art of teaching and have a strong foundation in your profession. However, the field of education is constantly evolving, and there are always new techniques, theories, and strategies to learn. To continue your professional development and enhance your teaching skills, it may be worth considering advanced degree programs and certifications in the field of teacher education.

Advanced degree programs, such as a master's or doctoral degree in education, provide an opportunity to delve deeper into educational theory, research, and practice. These programs offer specialized knowledge and advanced training in areas such as curriculum design, educational leadership, special education, or instructional technology. By pursuing an advanced degree, you can gain a deeper understanding of educational principles, engage in critical analysis of current practices, and develop expertise in a specific area of interest.

In addition to advanced degrees, certifications can also be valuable for experienced teachers looking to expand their skills and knowledge. Certifications are shorter, focused programs that allow you to gain expertise in a specific area of teaching. For example, you might consider obtaining a certification in teaching English as a second language (TESOL), special education, or educational technology. These certifications not only provide you with specialized knowledge but also demonstrate your commitment to professional growth and can enhance your job prospects.

When exploring advanced degree programs and certifications, it is important to consider your personal and professional goals. Reflect on the areas of teaching that interest you the most or the gaps in your current skillset that you would like to fill. Research different programs and certifications to find those that align with your interests and goals. Consider factors such as program duration, flexibility, cost, and reputation.

Furthermore, it is essential to evaluate the practicality of pursuing an advanced degree or certification while working as a teacher. Some programs offer flexible scheduling options, such as evening or online classes, to accommodate the needs of working professionals. Additionally, check if there are any financial aid or scholarship opportunities available to support your educational journey.

Ultimately, exploring advanced degree programs and certifications can take your teaching career to new heights. By continuing your professional development, you stay up-to-date with the latest research and practices in education, become more effective in the classroom, and open doors to new opportunities. So, take the time to explore the options available to you and embark on a journey of lifelong learning in the field of teacher education.

Making the Most of Professional Development Funds

In the ever-evolving field of education, professional development plays a crucial role in helping experienced teachers stay up-to-date with the latest teaching methodologies, technologies, and research. However, accessing quality professional development opportunities can often be a financial challenge. That's where professional development funds come into play – these are resources set aside by educational institutions or districts to support teachers in their continuous learning journey.

As a student pursuing a career in teacher education, it is essential to understand how to make the most of these professional development funds. This subchapter will guide you through some effective strategies to maximize the benefits of these resources.

The first step is to familiarize yourself with the policies and guidelines regarding professional development funds in your educational institution or district. Each institution may have its own set of rules, including the maximum amount of funds available, eligible activities, and application procedures. By being well-informed, you can ensure that you make the most appropriate and successful applications.

Next, it is crucial to identify your professional development needs and goals. Reflect on your teaching practice and areas where you would like to enhance your skills or explore new approaches. This self-assessment will help you target specific professional development opportunities that align with your objectives. Whether it's attending conferences, workshops, or online courses, having a clear focus will enable you to choose the most relevant and impactful activities.

Networking is another powerful tool to maximize professional development funds. Connect with other teachers in your institution or district who are also interested in professional growth. Collaborate with them to organize joint professional development activities, such as hosting a workshop or inviting a guest speaker. By pooling resources and sharing costs, you can stretch your professional development funds further and create an enriching experience for all participants.

Additionally, keep an eye out for external funding opportunities. Many organizations, foundations, and government agencies offer grants or scholarships specifically for teachers' professional development. Research and apply for these grants, as they can provide additional financial support for attending conferences, taking advanced courses, or conducting research.

Lastly, remember that professional development is not limited to attending events or courses. Engage in self-directed learning by reading educational literature, participating in online forums, or joining professional learning communities. These activities are often free or require minimal investment but can have a significant impact on your professional growth.

By understanding how to navigate and make the most of professional development funds, you can ensure that your continuous learning journey as an experienced teacher remains both enriching and financially sustainable.

Chapter 10: Sustaining Professional Growth Over Time

Developing a Lifelong Learning Mindset

In the field of education, the pursuit of knowledge and professional growth should never cease. As educators, we have a responsibility to foster a lifelong learning mindset within ourselves. This subchapter aims to guide students pursuing a career in teaching on how to cultivate this mindset and engage in continuous professional development.

A lifelong learning mindset is a commitment to ongoing personal and professional growth. It involves being open to new ideas, seeking out opportunities for learning, and reflecting on one's own practice. By embracing this mindset, teachers can stay current with the latest research and pedagogical techniques, allowing them to better meet the evolving needs of their students.

One of the key aspects of developing a lifelong learning mindset is the recognition that learning does not end with formal education. While initial teacher education programs provide a solid foundation, they are only the beginning of a lifelong journey. As new research emerges and educational practices evolve, it is crucial for teachers to engage in continuous learning to enhance their teaching skills.

There are several strategies that aspiring teachers can employ to develop a lifelong learning mindset. First and foremost, it is essential to cultivate a curiosity about teaching and learning. This curiosity can be nurtured by regularly reading educational literature, subscribing to professional journals, and attending conferences and workshops. Engaging in these activities will keep teachers well-informed about the latest trends and research in education.

Furthermore, seeking out opportunities for collaboration and mentorship can greatly contribute to professional growth. Connecting with experienced educators and engaging in dialogue about teaching practices can offer invaluable insights and perspectives. Additionally, joining professional associations or online communities can provide a platform for ongoing learning and networking.

Another crucial aspect of developing a lifelong learning mindset is self-reflection. Teachers should regularly reflect on their practice, identifying areas of strength and areas for improvement. This can be achieved through journaling, peer observations, or seeking feedback from students and colleagues. By reflecting on their teaching methods, educators can make informed decisions about the areas they need to focus on and set goals for growth.

In conclusion, developing a lifelong learning mindset is essential for aspiring teachers in the field of teacher education. By embracing a commitment to ongoing learning, staying curious, seeking out collaboration and mentorship opportunities, and engaging in self-reflection, teachers can continuously refine their practice and better serve their students. Remember, teaching is a dynamic profession, and a lifelong learning mindset is the key to mastering the art of teaching.

Embracing a Growth-Oriented Attitude

In the journey of becoming an exceptional teacher, one of the most valuable qualities you can possess is a growth-oriented attitude. This mindset not only fuels your personal and professional development but also sets the stage for creating a positive and engaging learning environment for your students. In this subchapter, we will explore the importance of embracing a growth-oriented attitude and how it can transform your teaching practice.

Teachers who adopt a growth-oriented attitude understand that learning is a lifelong process. They view challenges as opportunities for growth and are not afraid to step out of their comfort zones. Instead of settling for mediocrity, they continuously seek ways to improve their instructional techniques, classroom management skills, and subject knowledge. By cultivating this mindset, you can become a role model for your students, demonstrating the value of perseverance and the rewards of embracing new learning experiences.

A growth-oriented attitude also allows you to adapt to the ever-evolving landscape of education. As a teacher, you will encounter new methodologies, technologies, and theories throughout your career. Instead of resisting change, a growth-oriented attitude encourages you to embrace innovation and stay up-to-date with the latest research and best practices. By doing so, you can provide your students with a relevant and engaging learning experience that prepares them for the challenges of the future.

Furthermore, adopting a growth-oriented attitude fosters a classroom culture of continuous improvement. By modeling a love for learning, you inspire your students to become lifelong learners themselves. You create an environment where mistakes are seen as stepping stones to success, and feedback is welcomed as an opportunity for growth. By nurturing this mindset in your students, you empower them to take ownership of their education and become active participants in their own learning journey.

To embrace a growth-oriented attitude, it is crucial to engage in reflective practice. Take the time to reflect on your teaching practices, identifying areas for improvement and setting goals for professional development. Seek feedback from colleagues, mentors, and even your students, and be open to constructive criticism. Embrace professional development opportunities, such as workshops, conferences, and online courses, to expand your knowledge and skills.

In conclusion, embracing a growth-oriented attitude is essential for teachers seeking to master the art of teaching. By adopting this mindset, you not only foster personal and professional growth but also create a dynamic and engaging learning environment for your students. Embrace challenges, stay open to change, and continually seek opportunities for improvement. By doing so, you will become a transformative teacher who inspires a love for learning and equips students with the skills they need to succeed in the ever-changing world.

Mentorship and Leadership Opportunities for Experienced Teachers

Introduction:
As experienced teachers, you have already mastered the art of teaching and have a wealth of knowledge and skills to offer. However, the journey of professional development never truly ends. In this subchapter, we will explore the importance of mentorship and leadership opportunities for experienced teachers like yourselves. By taking on these roles, you can continue to grow both personally and professionally, while making a significant impact on the field of education.

The Power of Mentorship:
Mentorship is a powerful tool that allows experienced teachers to guide and support novice educators in their journey. By sharing your wisdom and experiences, you can help shape the next generation of teachers. Mentorship provides an opportunity for you to reflect on your own practices, refine your teaching techniques, and gain fresh perspectives. Moreover, it allows you to build strong relationships with colleagues and foster a culture of collaboration within your educational institution.

Becoming a Leader:
As an experienced teacher, you have the potential to become a leader in the field of education. Leadership opportunities can range from leading professional development workshops, presenting at conferences, or even serving on educational committees. By taking on these roles, you not only enhance your own professional growth but also inspire and motivate others. Your leadership can influence

educational policies, curriculum development, and teaching practices, making a lasting impact on students and future educators.

Benefits of Mentorship and Leadership: Engaging in mentorship and leadership opportunities offers a multitude of benefits for experienced teachers. Firstly, it provides a sense of fulfillment and purpose, as you contribute to the growth and success of fellow educators. Secondly, it allows for continuous learning and self-improvement, as you stay updated with the latest research and trends in education. Furthermore, mentorship and leadership roles enhance your professional reputation and open doors for career advancement. By taking on these responsibilities, you become a role model to your students and inspire them to become lifelong learners.

Conclusion:
Embracing mentorship and leadership opportunities is a natural progression in the journey of professional development for experienced teachers. By sharing your knowledge, guiding novice educators, and taking on leadership roles, you can continue to grow personally and professionally. Mentorship and leadership not only benefit you but also contribute to the overall improvement of education. Remember, as an experienced teacher, you have the power to shape the future of education and inspire others to become passionate and effective educators.

Conclusion: Embracing the Journey of Continuous Professional Development

As we come to the end of this book, "Mastering the Art of Teaching: Professional Development for Experienced Teachers," we hope that you, as students in the field of teacher education, have gained valuable insights into the importance of continuous professional development. Throughout this journey, we have explored various aspects of the teaching profession and the significance of ongoing growth and learning in becoming a masterful educator.

The world of education is constantly evolving, and as teachers, it is crucial to keep up with the latest research, methodologies, and technologies that can enhance our teaching practices. Continuous professional development allows us to stay current, adapt to new challenges, and meet the diverse needs of our students.

One of the key takeaways from this book is that professional development should not be seen as a one-time event but as an ongoing process. It is a journey that requires commitment, self-reflection, and a growth mindset. Embracing this journey means acknowledging that there is always room for improvement and that we can continuously enhance our teaching skills.

We have explored various avenues for professional development, such as attending conferences, workshops, and seminars. These opportunities provide valuable networking opportunities, allowing us to connect with fellow educators and learn from their experiences. Additionally, engaging in collaborative projects, joining professional organizations, and seeking mentorship can also contribute to our professional growth.

Furthermore, the importance of self-reflection and self-assessment cannot be overstated. Taking the time to critically analyze our teaching practices, seeking feedback from colleagues and students, and setting personal goals are essential steps in our professional development journey. By continuously assessing our strengths and weaknesses, we can identify areas that require improvement and make the necessary adjustments to become more effective educators.

In conclusion, embracing the journey of continuous professional development is vital for experienced teachers. It enables us to stay ahead of the curve, adapt to the changing demands of education, and ultimately provide the best learning experience for our students. As you embark on your own teaching careers, we encourage you to embrace this journey, remain open to new ideas, and commit to lifelong learning. Remember, the art of teaching is an ever-evolving practice, and by dedicating ourselves to continuous professional development, we can truly master this art.

www.ingramcontent.com/pod-product-compliance
Lightning Source LLC
Chambersburg PA
CBHW052228150726
48002CB00003B/1333